The Frog Prince

Retold by Margaret Nash
Illustrated by Justin Grassi

Once upon a time there was a princess who had a beautiful ball. It was gold like the sun. One hot day the princess went into the garden to play with her ball.

She threw the ball up into the air and put out her hands to catch it. But when she threw the ball again, it went up ... and up ... and up ... and then down ... down ... down ... SPLASH! It fell into the pond.

‘Oh no!’ said the princess.
‘My beautiful golden ball!’
She ran over to the pond but she could not see the ball. The pond was very black.

The princess was so sad that she sat down and began to cry.

Just then someone called out to her, 'What is it, Princess? Why are you crying?'

The princess looked up and saw a frog.
'My beautiful golden ball is in your pond,' she said. 'Please help me.'
'If I find it for you,' said the frog, 'will you play with me?'
'Yes,' said the princess, 'I will.'

So the frog
swam down
into the pond.

When he came up again he had
the ball in his mouth.
'Oh, thank you, thank you,'
said the princess.

'Now will you play with me?'
asked the frog.
The princess looked at the frog.
She didn't like his big mouth or
the big lump on his nose. She didn't
want to play with this ugly little frog.

So the princess said, 'I can't play with you now. I must go back to the palace for my tea.' And she ran off as fast as she could.

When the princess was having her tea
the little frog came up to the door.
'Little princess, little princess,'
he called. 'Please let me in.'

'Who is that?' asked the king.

'It is just an ugly little frog,' said the princess. 'I was playing with my ball today and it fell in the pond. The frog got it back for me.'

'Then he must be your friend,' said the king, and he went to open the door. The little frog came into the palace.

He jumped up on a chair, then he jumped up on to the table.

'Can I have some of your tea?'
asked the frog.
'No,' said the princess.
But the king got cross and said,
'Let him eat some of your tea.'

After tea the frog said, 'I want to sleep now. Can I sleep on your bed?'

'No,' said the princess.

Then the king got very cross.

'Let him sleep on your bed,' he said.

So the frog jumped on to the bed.

‘Will you kiss me goodnight?’
the frog asked the princess.
The princess was going to say, ‘No,’
but she saw the king looking cross.

So she shut her eyes
and gave the ugly
little frog a kiss.

When she opened her eyes again, it was not the frog that she saw but a prince. He had a big mouth and a big lump on his nose, but he had a big smile. And the princess liked him.